Betty and Veronica®

A Girl's Guide to the 'Comic' World of Dating

by Amy Helmes

CIDER MILL PRESS

BOOK PUBLISHERS

Magnetic Wisdom: Betty and Veronica

13-Digit ISBN: 978-1-933662-44-2
10-Digit ISBN: 1-933662-44-1

This book may be ordered by mail from the publisher.
Please include $3.50 for postage and handling.

Please support your local bookseller first!

Books published by Cider Mill Press Book Publishers are available at special discounts for bulk
purchases in the United States by corporations, institutions, and other organizations.
For more information, please contact the publisher.

Cider Mill Press Book Publishers
"Where good books are ready for press"
12 Port Farm Road
Kennebunkport, Maine 04046

Visit us on the web!
www.cidermillpress.com

Design by: Tilly Grassa, TGCreative Services
Package Cover Design by: Julie Reynolds

Printed in China
1 2 3 4 5 6 7 8 9 0
First Edition

Contents

Chapter 1
Friends (and Foes) Forever

Two beauties, both alike in dignity, in fair Riverdale where we lay our scene...

William Shakespeare may have cornered the market on drama when it comes to teen romance, but even the bard would be intrigued by the likes of Betty Cooper and Veronica Lodge. As the two dueling divas of the *Archie* comic book series, their borderline obsession for the same man keeps them forever locked in a rivalry of epic proportions.

Amidst the long but ongoing history of feuding female celebrities, Veronica and Betty represent the ultimate brunette vs. blonde face-off. With their catty remarks and acts of subtle sabotage, they've been at odds with each other for decades in the quest for Archie Andrews's heart. Yet remarkably, defying all laws of probability, they've managed to remain the best of friends through it all. (Their claws, it would seem, are retractable.)

When viewed as a microcosm for the real world, the idyllic town of Riverdale has all the ups, downs, windfalls and catastrophes of real life — especially when it comes to dating. From unwanted advances to unfulfilled infatuations, Betty and Veronica have loved, lost and then

some, alongside a colorful cast of cads and commitment-phobes. You'd think two of the most sought-after babes in high school would have the men in their lives all figured out. On the contrary, they're just as perplexed as ever. Yet matters of the heart have never managed to dampen their spirit, destroy their self-esteem or present more than a minor road bump in their friendship. Surely after 60 years of adolescence they'd have some wisdom to impart to the female masses about life, love and romantic entanglements (if not their secrets for maintaining that youthful glow)? Although Betty and Veronica are as different as day and night, together they've got the sort of girl power we should all strive for. It doesn't take a visionary to predict that Archie will never be able to choose one girl over the other. But in the end, maybe that's more *his* loss than theirs.

An Age-Old Dilemma: Good Girl Vs. Vixen

$\mathcal{S}$ome guys might call Archie the luckiest man on earth. With two gorgeous girls vying for his affection, the freckle-faced teen has spent more than half a century engaged in a manic game of relationship musical chairs. The guy is seriously torn about how to divvy up his affections for Betty and Veronica, two fetching young females of diverse nature but equal allure. Does he play it safe and choose Betty, the sweet-but-unsophisticated Donna Reed wannabe who moons over him like a lost puppy? Or, does he opt for Veronica, the gorgeous-but-spoiled drama queen who is full of passion — yet seems liable to break his heart?

Good girl or vixen? Sweetheart or siren? Blonde or brunette? It's the age-old debate, and one on which even readers of the Archie comics can never seem to agree. Over the years, devoted followers of the series have typically been divided into two camps: Those who think benevolent Betty is more worthy of Archie's love and those who believe that Archie can only truly be happy with a feisty dame like Veronica. In many ways, the girls are polar opposites, and yet they have an equal pull on Archie's heartstrings (in a very "tug-o-war" sense of the word).

Let's consider **Betty Cooper** for starters: Idealistic and upbeat, her disposition is almost always as sunny as her shiny flaxen ponytail. She's not at all stuck-up and is happy to befriend even the geekier segments of Riverdale society. By excelling at just about any endeavor she undertakes (be it cooking a gourmet meal or drag racing), Betty single-handedly shatters the "dumb blonde" myth. If her many talents don't prove threatening to her male counterparts, then her penchant for tomboy activities like athletics and auto mechanics sometimes have the unfortunate side effect of making her "one of the guys." Yet both her daydreams and the pages of her diaries reveal an incurable romantic. Fresh-faced and beautiful in a "girl-next-door" sort of

way, Betty is hopelessly devoted to Archie (and not exactly subtle in her overtures), but her naïve sensibilities can often leave her stranded in Veronica's shadow. She might fare better with Archie if she took a cue from her rival and played a little more hard-to-get, but how could she possibly put the kibosh on a crush that she's had since she was just a kid?

Veronica Lodge, on the other hand, knows how to land a man. In fact, she's gotten everything she's ever wanted since the day she was born with a silver spoon in her mouth. As the daughter of Riverdale's richest man, Veronica tools around town in luxury sports cars while dressed in the latest high-priced threads, making her the envy of girls for miles around.

She's got sass, class and plenty of style, and can be depended on to shop herself silly at the local mall. Although she loves being the center of attention, her oversize ego and sense of entitlement can sometimes be a turn-off. (You can thank her indulgent daddy and personal butler for that.) Perhaps it's her coquettish neediness that makes her attractive to Riverdale's eligible bachelors. Or maybe it's her "I can take you or leave you" vibe that really drives the men in her life bonkers. Veronica enjoys catty gossip almost as much as she loves to bask in her own self-flattery. And while she's not too elitist to shun interaction with her plebeian friends, she certainly takes the term "high maintenance" to stratospheric new levels.

The Art of War

Although they're often connected at the hip, routinely confide in each other and can practically finish each other's sentences, all bets are off between these two gal pals when it comes to romance. When your best friend has designs on the boy you covet, what's a girl to do?

Try a little sabotage, for starters. Both Betty and Veronica have been guilty of employing some clever schemes in their attempts to thwart each other, and their tactics would put the Army's Special Ops unit to shame. From tagging along "third wheel"-style on their rival's romantic night out to giving their opponent a hideous makeover to repel the opposite

sex, there's almost no ploy the girls haven't tried in their quest to outfox each other in the dating game. Quick to fire off an insult or a dagger-shooting stare, Betty and Veronica both subscribe to the theory that all's fair in love and war. But their animosity over "Archiekins" is peanuts compared to the tensions that flare any time these two beauties clash over clothing! (It's one thing to share a guy, after all, but showing up to the school dance in the same outfit? Not on your life!) When that happens, the kid gloves come off and teary-eyed tantrums ensue as both girls claim dress-wearing dibs with all the tenacity of two cold-war countries involved in a nuclear standoff.

Yet whether it's a crime of passion or fashion

that sets them at odds, their ongoing feuds always stop short of all-out viciousness. Archie's a catch, after all, but he's hardly worth ruining a friendship over. That said, for every grudge match in which they engage, the girls also have their moments of mutual *detente*. Not only do Betty and Veronica call a truce, they forge a fierce alliance when some other winsome beauty tries to put the moves on "their" man. Together, they'll team up to make sure that if neither of them can have Archie, no one else can either — and that goes double for Cheryl Blossom, the sexy seductress from another high school who is shameless in her attempts to steal Archie away. It's times like these when Veronica and Betty's friendship is at its most

Teflon-tough. After all, there's only room enough for *three* in this legendary love triangle.

Betty & Veronica: Through the Years

*T*here's something about teenage crushes that leaves us all feeling a little nostalgic. Regardless of whether you attended high school in the era of sock hops, sit-ins, punk rock or hip-hop, you'll probably always remember those boys who slipped love notes in your locker or slow-danced with you in the dimly lit, streamer-laden gymnasium. Across more than six decades, Betty and Veronica have adapted with changing fashions, fads, slang terminology and musical tastes. They've gone from dancing the jitterbug and

23

24

digging the Beatles (okay, make that "The Termites") to playing video games and even experimenting with the "Goth" look. But through it all, the one thing that has remained a constant in Betty and Veronica's darling teenage existence is their devotion to Archie — and to each other (Well...at least, *most* of the time).

We've learned from Betty that a positive attitude can take you far in life, and that girls can succeed in anything they put their mind to. Veronica's taught us that shopping is an art, and although money may not buy you love, it can definitely buy you a killer wardrobe. Together, they've exemplified the thrill of dating victory and the agony of dating defeat, and have shown us that love — even in the pages of a comic book — is one seriously complicated endeavor.

As they forever fumble through their teenage years with an eye toward finding true romance, Veronica and Betty represent surprisingly realistic icons of female friendship. Yes, their relationship is fraught with friction, but no matter how much they push each other's buttons, they're always ready to forgive and forget. As competitive as they may be in their "boy crazy" endeavors, they're loyal to each other when it matters most. They've even grudgingly learned to share Archie (although neither of them finds this arrangement ideal, to put it mildly).

Time stands still when you're having fun,

and at the rate they're going, Betty and Veronica won't ever graduate from Riverdale High, let alone get anything approximating a marriage proposal from Archie. But perhaps there's just as much to be learned from the thrill of the chase as there is in the happily-ever-after. If you can conjure up even a fraction of Betty and Veronica's adolescent enthusiasm, it might just add a bit more color to your future dating adventures — and keep you forever young at heart.

Chapter 2

The Riverdale Rules of Attraction

Are the guys you date more cartoonish than you'd care to admit? Perhaps acquainting yourself with the young men Betty and Veronica encounter every day might help you better understand your own potential mates. From boys-next-door to beefcakes, bookworms and billionaires, there's a type of suitor to suit just about any girl's fancy. Sure, Riverdale's resident heartthrobs can be exasperating, foolish and a bit two-dimensional at times. But when it matters most, they'll win you over with their swoon-worthy good looks, unique charm and endearing personalities. Since dating is never without its comic moments, look to Archie and his cohorts to help you navigate the madcap world of men. If you're still left scratching your head, don't despair: It's taken Betty and Veronica six decades and counting to figure these guys out!

The Type: Archie Andrews

Why You'll Love Him: There's something about an all-American boy that leaves women smitten like kittens. In Betty and Veronica's case, Archie is the guy with whom they both dream of some day walking off into the sunset, preferably

attired in full bridal regalia (haute couture in Ronnie's case). Archie is cute (but not cocky), funny (but not a dork) and friendly (but not in a "Let's just be friends," sort of way). By the same token, he's not *so* perfect as to make a girl feel inadequate, having just enough foibles and unpolished edges to make him semi-attainable. He's loyal to his buds — of which he has plenty, and if all that weren't enough, he's also got the chick-magnet ace-in-the-hole: his own rock band. And you wonder why Veronica and Betty *both* want a piece of him?

Relationship Pitfalls: Fall for an "Archie" and you'd better be willing to share him. This guy's less capable of commitment than a fickle ice cream aficionado trying to choose from 31 flavors. Of course, Archie has a decent excuse for wanting to play the field: He's only seventeen years old! Still, his roving eye and penchant for dating more than one girl at a time makes us skeptical that he'll ever settle down. When hot-to-trot bombshell Cheryl Blossom saunters into a room with her "Va-va-va-voom" good looks, it's all Archie can do to keep from salivating while Betty and Veronica seethe in a jealous rage. Rest assured, if there's a bikini-clad girl within gawking distance, an Archie boy will be checking out the goods.

Tips For Dating an "Archie": Whether through his own impulsiveness or at the behest of an ill-advised friend, Archie has a habit of getting into a pickle, often entangling his "date du jour" in these madcap misadventures. For this reason, your parents might not approve of your dating an "Archie," much like Veronica's father, who is less-than-keen on his daughter's crush. But since when have you been attracted to the boys that your parents sanction? Besides, an Archie guy has never met an obstacle he couldn't use his good looks and charm to overcome. Just when you think he's toast, he always lands butter-side up.

Classic Archie Moment: After inadvertently promising both Betty and Veronica a New Year's Eve kiss at the stroke of midnight, Archie was saved from his dilemma at the eleventh (make that twelfth) hour, when Jughead's dog slobbered all over his face. A grossed-out Veronica refused to kiss a boy whose lips had touched a dog's lips. Betty, on the other hand, was more than willing to accept the second smooch and happily puckered up!

The Type: Jughead Jones (a.k.a. Forsythe Pendleton Jones)

Why You'll Love Him: If you're into skinny, eccentric guys with a truly bizarre sense of humor, Jughead may well be your perfect match. Always one to swim against the stream, he could be considered the "indie hipster" of Archie's gang. His quirky and quixotic approach to life will keep

you amused on dates (at the very least, you won't be bored). And while his antics can be plenty outrageous, he typically has the chilled-out demeanor of a Tibetan monk, making you wonder if he's really more of a genius than his goofball persona would suggest.

Relationship Pitfalls: Just because he

wears that ridiculous crown everywhere he goes (including the prom) doesn't necessarily give Jughead "Prince Charming" status. While this type of guy never met a hamburger he didn't like, he's not as overt in his love for the opposite sex. Indeed, he occasionally acts as though merely saying hello to a girl could put him at risk for contracting the bubonic plague. He can be aloof and cynical, perhaps attributable to having had his heart broken once in some devastating fashion. (And what woman can resist a wounded soul?)

Tips For Dating a "Jughead": You can judge a guy's merits by the way he treats his sister, and in Jughead's case, he couldn't be sweeter to his baby sister, Jellybean. Should you come across a chap who reminds you of this tall drink of water, remember that he's less likely to ask you on a date than he is to ask you for a plate of brownies. So if you're too shy to ask *him* out, why not consider the latter? After all, the way to this man's heart is definitely through his stomach. But be forewarned: You might begrudge his ability to gorge on food for hours without gaining an ounce.

Classic Jughead Moment: Jughead is so averse to gentlemanly behavior that he once took Veronica to a dance and gave her a corsage made out of poison ivy.

The Type: Reggie Mantle

Why You'll Love Him: As the "alpha male" of Archie's gang, Reggie's cocky good looks and confident swagger make him one of the more popular guys in Riverdale (at least, in *his* opinion). Working a room like a politician, he'll go to great lengths to get what he wants, even if a bit of chicanery is required. Men of the "Reggie" regiment tend to have fat bank accounts, are slick with the ladies, and their bad-boy personas can be seriously hot. (Think Iceman from *Top Gun.*) If you've ever dreamed of dating a star athlete, then this big man on campus has certainly got game. Just be careful he doesn't play *you*!

Relationship Pitfalls: Although this bachelor isn't shy about chasing after girls, his number one love is himself. Whether staring longingly into a mirror or hiring his own groupies to fawn over him, Reggie's complete lack of humility can prove trying at times. So, too, can the fact that despite his family's wealth, he can be a total tightwad. Don't be surprised if a "Reggie" boy expects you to go Dutch on a date — or demands you reimburse him gas money. If you're looking for a Sugar Daddy, you'd best look elsewhere.

Tips For Dating a "Reggie": A little ego stroking will go a heck of a long way toward winning this guy's favor. Humor his passion for athletics (he's psycho competitive), and treat him like royalty, if not a minor deity. When dating a "Reggie," you'll have to develop a thick skin; his snarky 'tude and penchant for playing cruel practical jokes may at times have you feeling more like his emotional punching bag than his girlfriend. Still, when you consider that Betty and Veronica still associate with Reggie after all the grief he's given them, he must have some redeeming qualities to compensate for his overt megalomania.

Classic Reggie Moment: Dressed as Darth Vader, Reggie so wanted to win the school's costume contest that he sabotaged Archie's get-up while his rival took a shower. Reggie still ended up losing, however, when Archie used an old trashcan to craft an R2-D2 costume that took first place.

The Type: Dilton Doiley

Why You'll Love Him: Think a guy's most attractive feature is his brain? In that case, Riverdale's resident egghead, Dilton, could turn your knees to jelly. The bespectacled brainiac has a MacGyver-like ability to solve problems, often with jaw-droppingly cool inventions like androids and time machines. There's something strangely hot about a guy who sports this much brainpower. Because let's face it: In the end, it's always the class nerd who ends up being the next Bill Gates.

Relationship Pitfalls: Whether he's spouting off Latin truisms or running statistical analyses, a "Dilton" boy can be a little too erudite for his own good. (If you don't know the meaning of "erudite," consider your name officially deleted from his dating database.) You'll either be bored to tears or totally perplexed when he enthuses about his passion for cryptozoology or tinkers on his computer mainframe for hours at a time. Doesn't he realize that you'd rather be snuggling on the sofa with him? It only goes to show that while he may know a lot, there's one thing he'll never understand: the workings of the female mind.

Tips For Dating a "Dilton": A boy of Dilton's demeanor judges a girl by the size of her ... IQ. Unless you've got the cerebral *chutzpah* of Dilton's erstwhile crush, Danni Malloy, he may never deem you worthy enough to be the "E" to his "mc-squared." So until you've acquired a doctorate degree in aerospace engineering, can solve a Rubik's cube in under a minute or can (at the very least) hum the theme song from *Jeopardy*, don't expect a man of this intellectual ilk to give you the time of day.

Classic Dilton Moment: Hoping to "cure" Betty of her obsession with Archie, Dilton used classic psychological treatments like aversion therapy, hypnosis and tapping the subconscious to rid the redhead from her mind. (It didn't work.)

The Type: Moose
(a.k.a Marmaduke Mason)

Why You'll Love Him: At first glance he's nothing but a big lug — a rocks-for-brains doofus looking for his next meal or physical confrontation (not necessarily in that order). But once you get to know him, this brawny behemoth shows an earnest naïveté that is completely disarming. When he sticks up for the class geek or uses his brute strength to protect you from danger, you'll realize that this type of guy is far more teddy bear than T-Rex. He's got a heart as big as his biceps, and he'll always defend your honor, even if it means serving someone a knuckle sandwich.

Relationship Pitfalls: If you're looking for deep, meaningful conversation, count this guy out. (Considering most of his sentences start with 'D-uh,' he's not exactly a seasoned intellectual.) Yet his more alarming character flaw is an out-of-control possessiveness that takes hold of him with a Hulk-like tenacity. When another man so much as looks at Moose's girlfriend, Midge, he turns seriously aggro. So say goodbye to any platonic relationship you might have with another guy — a "Moose" man might misconstrue your friendship and put him in a half nelson.

Tips For Dating a "Moose": There's no need to dismiss a guy out of hand simply because he's not as smart as you. In Moose's case, it's dyslexia that has long tripped him up in the world of academia. Offer to be his private tutor and he may soon be tutoring you in the art of romance. Just don't make the mistake of thinking that his scholastic failings keep him up at night. Moose thinks his straight "Fs" stand for "Fantastic." As they say, ignorance is bliss.

Classic Moose Moment: Moose burst into tears when he mistakenly believed he had ripped Archie's arm out of its socket. In reality, it was just a fake arm Archie had worn to teach the bully a lesson.

Chapter 3
Betty & Veronica's Dating Do's and Don'ts

ating can at times be so complicated that it really ought to come with an instruction manual. While navigating love's labyrinth of social rules and regulations, consider the wisdom set forth from Riverdale's own romance experts. Betty and Veronica have certainly had their fair share of dating disasters over the years, but if you take the time to learn from their mistakes, perhaps you won't be doomed to repeat them. Here are a few important "Do's" and "Don'ts" to keep in mind on your quest for love:

Don't experiment drastically with your look before a big event.

There's a time and place for trying out a new image, but the day before a much-anticipated romantic rendezvous isn't the best opportunity for attempting an extreme makeover. Wanting to glam it up for her date with "international playboy" Dexter Van Dann, Veronica got the bright idea to experiment with an elaborately beaded, braided hairstyle. Not only did the complicated 'do cost $400 and take 12 hours to create, it also didn't win her any favors with Dex. She was forced to decline his invitation to go water skiing rather than risk getting her high-maintenance hairstyle wet. In the end, Dexter took Betty out on his boat instead, leaving Ronnie stewing on the shore.

Do introduce your boyfriend to your parents in a casual, comfortable setting where everyone will feel at ease.
Meeting your folks can be incredibly nerve-wracking for a guy, so try to keep their first

introduction light and informal. When Veronica took Archie to a hoity-toity French café to meet her dad, her new beau felt awkward and extremely out of his element in such a classy joint, where he couldn't even read the menu. Archie always feels equally ill at ease in Veronica's colossal mansion, where his clumsiness occasionally proves his downfall around Mr. Lodge's priceless antiques. If Archie can break things so easily, the millionaire is naturally skeptical that his daughter's heart won't be next!

Don't assume that boys don't make passes at girls who wear glasses.
Veronica mocked Betty when she showed up at school in a pair of spectacles, only to eat

her words when the school's cutest preppie boy started flirting with her four-eyed friend. Of course, Veronica scrambled to find her own pair of glasses, despite the fact that she had 20/20 vision.

The too-strong prescription made her unwittingly hit on the middle-aged principal, Mr. Weatherbee, which, needless to say, proved exceedingly mortifying for both parties.

Do be wary of men bearing gifts.

It's always sweet when a guy shows up for a date with flowers or a box of chocolate. But when Jughead once concocted his own nail polish recipe for Veronica, she was alarmed to later find out that his formula was highly explosive and much sought after by the Pentagon! (The lesson here? Boys and cosmetics don't mix!)

Don't get your hopes up before meeting a blind date.

While it's easy to let your imagination run wild when arranging to meet a guy sight unseen, it's usually better to keep your expectations in check. Veronica dropped Archie like a hot potato and agreed to let Jughead's cousin, Melvin, escort her to a school dance after hearing that he was a male model. Although she had imagined he'd be a real dreamboat, her hopes sank faster than the *Titanic* when she saw her date's none-too-attractive features and learned he was actually only a foot model for a corn medication company. Needless to say, Veronica wished *she'd* have been blind on this particular date!

*D*o *think twice before dating a celebrity.* Betty learned this rule the hard way when she fell for "The Boss," Bruce Bingstone, back in the mid-'80s. The singer took a shine to the perky blonde, but she soon found he wasn't worth the effort when they had to hide in trashcans to escape the notice of his obsessive, stalker fans. Not exactly "glory days" for Betty — by the time he left town the next day, she was relieved to be rid of him.

Don't assume that fidelity is a given.
Women sometimes have the tendency to read more than they should into a guy's romantic gestures. When Archie gave Betty his class ring, she naturally presumed they were finally going steady. But when Veronica snidely showed off the class pin *she'd* gotten from Archie, both girls were seeing red. Feeling mutually

betrayed, Veronica and Betty ultimately forced Archie to choose one of them by competing for his affection in a kissing contest. (Why do we get the impression that Archie walked away the *real* winner in this scenario?)

Do be yourself. Although it may be tempting to impress a guy by putting on airs, he'd much rather get to know the real you. After overhearing Archie say that he liked Veronica because she had couth, Betty

transformed herself into a sophisticated diva in the hopes that she'd get more play with her crush. When she walked around town

with the upturned nose of a snooty socialite, Archie turned his nose up at *her*, saying he preferred girls who just acted like themselves.

Don't bleed a guy's bank account dry. If the price of dating you is too high, you may "emotionally bankrupt" a prospective boyfriend.

On one of her first dates with Archie, Veronica expected him to wear a tuxedo and take her to the ritzy El Crocodearo supper club. Yet the only way Archie could afford this pricey date was to simultaneously work in the restaurant as a busboy, which needless to say, left Veronica at a "table for one" for most of the evening. Had she expected less, she might have gotten more in the way of romance.

Do play hard to get — at least occasionally. Economically speaking, when you limit supply, demand will increase. Dating works the same way. Make yourself "unavailable" and sometimes, you'll make a guy clamor for you even more. When Archie asked Betty out (after first asking Veronica and getting shot down), Betty gave him the cold shoulder — literally — by dumping her ice cream sundae on his head and announcing that she wouldn't play second fiddle. Sometimes, guys need to be reminded that a woman's pride should not be trifled with.

Don't put up with ridiculous male machismo. Taking his cue from a "Fonzee"-like figure, Archie once donned a leather jacket, straddled a motorcycle and tried to act all "tough guy" with the girls. He talked down to them and treated them callously, thinking his devil-may-care attitude would make them swoon. Rather than fall for his rebel persona,

Veronica and Betty rightly blasted him for being a jerk.

Do be willing to shatter traditional gender roles. Not all guys dig girly-girls, so

don't be afraid to let your tomboyish traits shine through. Every time Archie's car breaks down on a date with Betty, she comes to his rescue by popping the hood of his car and fixing the problem (all without managing to

64

get even one grease stain on her dress!). It only goes to show that there's more than one way to rev a guy's engine!

Don't be a slave to fashion.
Generally speaking, guys are unimpressed by designer labels. Case in point, when Veronica once wore a diamond studded, 24-karat gold "Oscar de la Hautedawg" cowbell around her neck in the hopes that other girls would copy her style, the guys at school ridiculed her resemblance to a farm animal. (Not exactly the reaction Ronnie was hoping for.)

Do know when to make a guy eat his heart out.

Feeling underappreciated by your man? Try recruiting the green-eyed monster to help teach him a lesson. When Archie and Jughead snubbed Betty and Veronica during a fishing outing, the girls were miffed —until they later ended up reeling in two gorgeous camp counselors. You

can bet the girls paraded their fabulous "catches" in front of Archie and Jughead. The moral of this story? There are plenty of fish in the sea.

Don't spend too much time primping for a guy.
Men can never fully appreciate
the amount of effort
women put into their
looks, so sometimes,
it's better to not
even try. Feeling
totally embarrassed
by her unkempt appear-
ance when Archie dropped by
her house on cleaning day, Betty ran to her
room to get dolled-up. Not only was he
sleeping when she finally reappeared wearing
her best dress, but he also had the audacity to
point out that Veronica owned a dress exactly
like hers. So much for compliments!

Chapter 4

Desperately Seeking. . .

*C*ontrary to what their ongoing Archie alterca-
tions might imply, Veronica and Betty are
boy-crazy dating machines. You won't catch them
sitting home on a Friday night languishing for the
one that got away when there are so many hotties
in town to have fun with in the meantime. Since
the girls have managed to keep up with the
changing trends across more than half a century
of dating, what better way to continue their
search for Mr. Right (okay, Mr. Right *Now*) than by

employing the most modern method available: online dating? Here's how their Internet profiles might shape up:

Betty's Dating Profile

Online handle: Ain't_She_Sweet?

Age: 17

Hair color: Blonde

Physique: Fit and athletic

Resides in: East Riverdale

Favorite hangouts: Pop Tate's Chock'lit Shoppe, the beach, the mall

Personal motto: "Blondes have more fun."

Role models: Betty Crocker, Mother Teresa, Danielle Steele

Celebrity I most resemble: Hilary Duff

Hobbies: Cooking, sewing, baseball, journal writing, cheerleading and volunteer work.

Prized possession: A high school football jersey that still bears the faint scent of its original owner. (sigh)

Turn-ons: Red-hair, freckles, guys in bands

Turn-offs: Flakiness, mean spiritedness, slobs and snobs

About me:

$\mathcal{I}$ am a down-to-earth, fun-loving straight-A student with no pretensions (unlike *some* people I know). I always wear my heart on my sleeve, but if that's not enough, you'll know what I'm thinking by the thought bubbles that follow me everywhere I go. I have lots of energy and enjoy nature and outdoor activities (including, but not limited to, long walks on the beach). I have lots of empathy for others because I know what it's like to be the odd woman out. When I fall in love, I fall hard — no soft landings for this girl! My tastes and my lifestyle may be simple, but rest assured, my heart is pure gold!

My ideal match:

$\mathcal{I}$'m looking for a "Prince Charming" who is interested in a committed relationship with long-term potential. Players and "serial daters" need not apply! If you can write me romantic poetry or love letters, I'll treat you in turn by baking you cookies or tuning up your car. I'd like a boyfriend who isn't threatened by my various skills and talents — after all, I'm just a regular girl (notwithstanding my "Super Teen" alter ego). Must have loads of integrity and be able to admit that cheerleading is, indeed, a real sport.

Veronica's Dating Profile

Online handle: Diva2Worship

Age: 17

Hair color: Ravishing raven black

Physique: Stunningly perfect

Resides in: North Riverdale

Favorite hangouts: Parisian fashion houses, makeup counters, in front of mirrors

Personal motto: "Diamonds are a girl's best friend."

Role models: Coco Chanel, Cleopatra, Jacqueline Kennedy Onassis

Celebrity I most resemble: Liz Taylor (the early years)

Hobbies: Shopping, gossiping, starting new trends

Prized possession: My luxury sports car and personal ATM machine

Turn-ons: Compliments, private jets, the ring of a cash register

Turn-offs: Dollar stores, part-time jobs, and gentlemen who prefer blondes

About me:

*D*on't hate me because I'm beautiful...I was just born that way! In addition to my stunning features (as evidenced by my photo), I have class, couth and a commanding sense of style. I'm a lady through-and-through and expect to be treated as such. I'm also used to getting what I want. My friends find me to be honest — sometimes brutally so. I don't mince words, but am loyal and magnanimous to friends and servants alike. Just because I'm a woman of independent means doesn't make me a slacker; I have big ambitions to one day take over as CEO of my daddy's business (and I intend to be one of the best-dressed corporate raiders around). Despite my "comfortable" lifestyle, I'm also not afraid to slum it with the regular folks. Just don't expect me to go camping, clean toilets or wear knock-off clothes. Ewww!

My ideal match:

$\mathcal{I}$'m in the market for a man who has the sophistication to hang out in my rarified social circles without looking like a common peasant. Must be independently wealthy or have seven-figure salary potential. Should be comfortable hanging out in shopping malls holding my purse while I try on racks of clothes in the dressing room. I want a man who doesn't insist on being the center of attention — that's my job! My suitable match will be nice, but not so nice that he doesn't enjoy a good gossip session. In short, you can do no better than me. (Note: Email responses are subject to a rigorous screening process by my personal assistant.)

Chapter 5

Quiz:

Who's Your Comic Book Counterpart?

Want to know where you'd fit among Riverdale's bevy of babes? Take this personality test to determine whether you're most like Veronica, Betty or one of their notorious gal pals.

1) When I meet a cute guy, my first response is to:

a. Ask what tax bracket he's in.

b. Saunter past him with a seductive strut.

c. Flash a genuine smile and introduce myself.

d. Stalk him.

e. Warn him that I've already got a boyfriend.

2) One job I might be interested in is:

a. Taking over the family business.

b. Swimsuit model.

c. Auto mechanic.

d. Bounty hunter.

e. Anger management counselor.

3) Which of the following describes your fashion sense?

a. Label fiend.
b. Barely there.
c. Conservative, but cute.
d. Whatever fits my lanky frame.
e. Anything that matches my boyfriend's letterman jacket.

4) I like a guy who...

a. Drives an expensive sports car.
b. Will dump his girlfriend for me.
c. I can envision living "happily ever after" with.
d. Plays hard to get.
e. Has a strong, muscular physique.

5) Which of the following best describes you?

a. Sophisticated.

b. Flirtatious.

c. Friendly.

d. Persistent.

e. Spoken for.

6) My idea of a perfect date would involve:

a. Champagne and caviar.

b. Lots of necking.

c. Dinner and a movie.

d. Not getting stood up!

e. A guy who can read the menu.

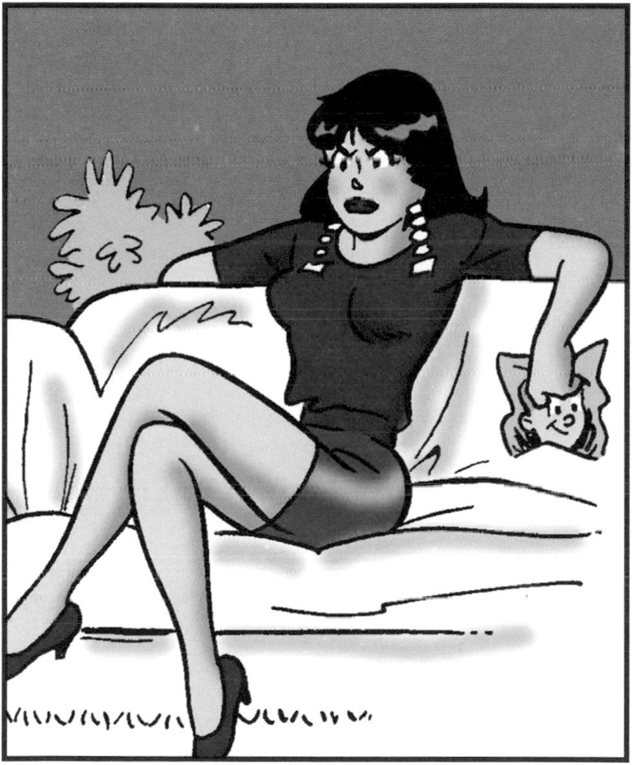

7) I'm not impressed by guys who:

a. Clip coupons.

b. Don't give me their undivided attention.

c. Get into trouble.

d. Aren't very unique.

e. Study a lot.

8) The movie that might best describe me is:

a. *Bonfire of the Vanities.*

b. *10*

c. *America's Sweetheart.*

d. *Funny Girl.*

e. *Married to the Mob.*

9) When a guy is jerk to me I usually:
a. Tell him off and storm angrily out of the room.
b. Choose from the 20 other guys waiting to take his place.
c. Vent about it in my journal.
d. End up liking him even more.
e. Have my boyfriend "take care of it."

10) You're liable to find me reading:
a. The *Forbes* annual list of wealthiest people.
b. A lingerie catalogue.
c. A romance novel.
d. *He's Just Not That Into You.*
e. *Sports Illustrated.*

11) My car of choice would be a:

a. Jaguar.

b. Convertible (i.e., something "topless").

c. Dependable American car.

d. Volkswagon Bug.

e. Humvee.

12) In my childhood, I often could be found:

a. Playing dress-up and raiding my mother's makeup kit.

b. Stealing my playmates' doll babies.

c. Concocting confections in my Easy-Bake oven.

d. Pestering the boys in my neighborhood.

e. Holding onto an overstuffed teddy bear.

13) What historical figure would you most like to meet?

a. Gianni Versace.

b. Mae West.

c. (Princess) Grace Kelly.

d. Sadie Hawkins.

e. Attila the Hun.

14) The motto I most adhere to is:

a. "He who dies with the most toys wins."

b. "If you've got it, flaunt it."

c. "Do unto others as you would have them do unto you."

d. "If at first you don't succeed, try, try again."

e. "Brawn before brains."

15) If I won the lottery, I'd probably:

a. Yawn. (Lottery money is chump change.)

b. Pay an agent to secure me a movie deal.

c. Give half of my earnings to charity.

d. Attempt to buy the affection of the man
   I love.

e. Buy a professional football team.

Tally Your Results...

...If you picked mostly "a"s, you're a Veronica Lodge

Madonna wasn't kidding. We *are* living in a material world. Like Riverdale's wealthy heiress, you have a lot to offer men, but it comes with a hefty price tag. You'll give a guy your attention only if he's got the stock port-folio and savoir-faire to make your champagne wishes and caviar dreams come true. Your posh style and attitude sets you apart from the crowd, but your

90

spoiled princess pout takes center stage when you don't get what you want. As far as you're concerned, you certainly can judge a book by its cover — and you'd take fine Corinthian leather over a cheap paperback any day!

...If you picked mostly "b"s, you're a Cheryl Blossom

When you walk into a room, you *own* it. Perhaps that's because you're comfortable in your own skin and have sex appeal in spades. Just as smokin' hot Cheryl can make the boys of

Riverdale do a double-take, guys line up at your feet in homage to your bodacious beauty. Sadly, your female friends are few and far between; girls are just too jealous of your feminine wiles to ever count you among their clique. But it's no matter — you prefer the company of men anyway!

...If you picked mostly "c"s, you're a
Betty Cooper
Sugar, spice and every-thing nice...You're a good girl whose modesty and concern for others means you have a lot in common with Archie's favorite blonde.

You have an independent spirit, you rarely complain, and you're loaded with talent (although far be it from you to toot your own horn). Still, nothing would make you happier than someday having the house, husband, 2.5 kids and white picket fence you've always dreamed of. Underneath all that common sense, you're a starry-eyed romantic at heart.

...If you picked mostly "d"s, you're an Ethel Muggs You march to the beat of your own drummer and are attracted to men who are similarly unorthodox,

to put it mildly. While you've never been as lucky in love as you'd like, you're not the sort to let a little rejection stand in the way of true love (even if it's currently the unrequited kind). Like Jughead Jones's No. 1 groupie, the only thing that could prevent you from going after what you want is a court-sanctioned restraining order. After all, you believe "No" is just a synonym for "Not today, but maybe tomorrow."

...If you picked mostly "e"s, you're a
Midge Klump

When it comes to love, you prefer a burly man to a girly man. The guy who captures your fancy is someone who could open the stubborn lid on a peanut butter jar *and* save you from a band of brigands (because we know how prevalent brigands are these days). Forget

interesting conversation — you want a Russell-Crowe-in-*Gladiator* type of guy, complete with ripped torso, bulging biceps and broad shoulders. Once you find him, your heart will never stray. Good thing, too, 'cause the guys you date aren't into "open" relationships.